BLAZERS

MILITARY VEHICLES

U.S.
AIR FORCE

SPY PLANES

by Carrie A. Braulick

Reading Consultant:
Barbara J. Fox
Reading Specialist
North Carolina State University

Capstone
press®

Mankato, Minnesota

Blazers is published by Capstone Press,
151 Good Counsel Drive, P.O. Box 669, Mankato, Minnesota 56002.
www.capstonepress.com

Library of Congress Cataloging-in-Publication Data
Braulick, Carrie A., 1975–
     U.S. Air Force spy planes / by Carrie A. Braulick.
     p. cm.—(Blazers. Military vehicles)
     Summary: "Describes spy planes, their design, equipment, weapons, crew,
missions, and role in the U.S. Air Force"—Provided by publisher.
     Includes bibliographical references and index.
     ISBN-13: 978-0-7368-6453-4 (hardcover)
     ISBN-10: 0-7368-6453-9 (hardcover)
     1. Reconnaissance aircraft—United States—Juvenile literature. 2. United
States. Air Force—Juvenile literature. I. Title. II. Series.
     UG1242.R4B73 2007
     623.74′670973—dc22   2006002795

Editorial Credits
Martha E. H. Rustad, editor; Thomas Emery, designer; Jo Miller,
     photo researcher/photo editor

Photo Credits
Check Six/Brian Shul, 8; George Hall, 4–5, 28–29
DVIC/Master Sgt. Rose Reynolds, 10–11; SSGT Jeffrey A. Wolfe, 26–27 (top);
     SSGT Suzanne M. Jenkins, 20–21
Photo by Ted Carlson/Fotodynamics, cover, 6–7, 18, 22–23, 26–27 (bottom)
U.S. Air Force photo, 19; Airman 1st Class Brandi Branch, 24–25; Capt. John
     Sheets, 13 (top); Master Sgt. Deb Smith, 9 (top); Master Sgt. Rob Valenca,
     15; Senior Airman Shaun Emery, 9 (bottom); Staff Sgt. Cohen Young, 13
     (bottom); Staff Sgt. Matthew Hannen, 14; Staff Sgt. Suzanne M. Jenkins,
     16–17

**Capstone Press thanks Dr. Ray Puffer, Historian, Edwards Air Force Base,
     for his assistance with this book.**

1 2 3 4 5 6 11 10 09 08 07 06

TABLE OF CONTENTS

AIR FORCE SPY PLANES

Enemies of the United States think they have a lot of secrets. But they don't know when a U.S. Air Force spy plane is flying over and watching them.

Spy planes keep track of enemies day and night. They fly missions over faraway countries.

The main Air Force spy plane is the U-2. The Predator also goes on spying missions. This small plane has no pilot inside. Crews on the ground use controls to fly the Predator.

U-2 SPY PLANE

PREDATOR

PREDATOR GROUND CONTROL STATION

DESIGN

Spy planes fly high to stay safe from enemy weapons. The lightweight body of the U-2 flies up to 15 miles (24 kilometers) above the ground.

Spy planes carry some of the best cameras ever made. U-2 cameras take photos from up to 100 miles (160 kilometers) away. Predators carry cameras that even work in the dark.

BLAZER FACT

The Predator was built in 1994. It was the Air Force's first unmanned spy plane. By using the Predator, pilots stay safe from enemy weapons.

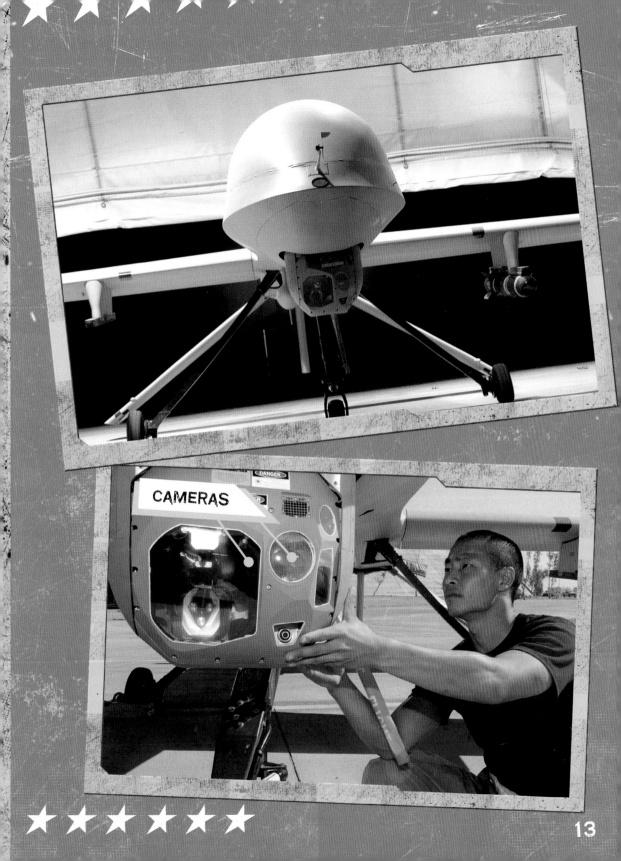

CAMERAS

U-2s have powerful engines that need a lot of fuel to keep running. The engines keep the planes in the air for their long missions. Predators have smaller engines that use less fuel.

BLAZER FACT

U-2 pilots carry tubes filled with high-energy food to eat during missions that can last up to 7 hours.

WEAPONS AND EQUIPMENT

U-2s don't carry weapons. But Predators can carry powerful missiles. These missiles blast holes in strong enemy vehicles.

MISSILE

Controls and screens fill the U-2 cockpit. Pilots watch display screens to see objects in the sky around them, especially at night.

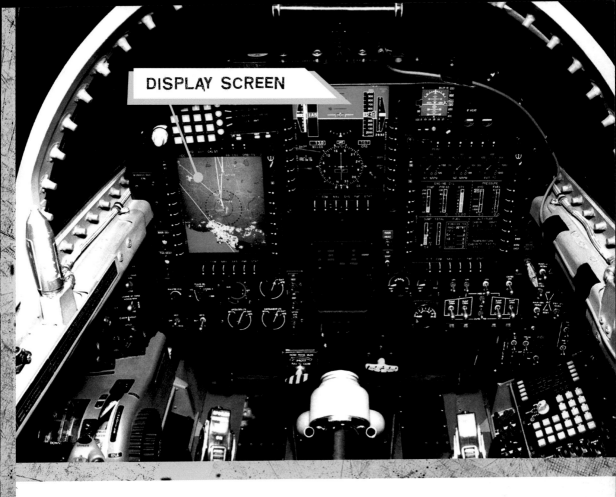

DISPLAY SCREEN

BLAZER FACT

Pilots use information from the U-2 radar to make detailed maps of the mission area.

TOWER: 0322/0503

RAPCON: 0261

WX: 0487
B-DOCK X0605 0600

Spy plane sensors work with satellite systems. The sensors send pictures to people in the control center. The pictures arrive in less time than it takes to snap your fingers!

U-2 DIAGRAM

TAIL

WING

COCKPIT

NOSE

FUEL TANK

EYES IN THE SKY

The higher planes fly, the harder it is for pilots to breathe. U-2 pilots wear pressure suits. The oxygen that is pumped into the suits helps pilots breathe while in thin air.

★ ★ ★ ★ ★ ★

Spy planes give information to the military to help them make good decisions. With each new photo, there is another chance to stop enemies in their tracks.

BLAZER FACT

Pilots fly U-2s over areas hurt by earthquakes, floods, and other natural disasters. These missions help rescuers find injured people.

GLOSSARY

missile (MISS-uhl)—an explosive weapon that can travel long distances

mission (MISH-uhn)—a military task

oxygen (OK-suh-juhn)—a colorless gas in the air; humans and animals need oxygen to breathe.

pressure suit (PRESH-ur SOOT)—clothing worn by pilots to protect them when they fly very high

satellite system (SAT-uh-lite SISS-tuhm)—equipment that gathers data from instruments that orbit the earth

sensor (SEN-sur)—an instrument that can detect changes and send the information to a controlling device

unmanned plane (UHN-mand PLANE)—a flying vehicle that carries no people and is controlled from the ground

READ MORE

Doeden, Matt. *The U.S. Air Force.*
The U.S. Armed Forces. Mankato, Minn.:
Capstone Press, 2005.

Donovan, Sandra. *The U.S. Air Force.*
Minneapolis: Lerner, 2005.

Green, Michael, and Gladys Green. *Remotely Piloted Aircraft: The Predators.* War Machines. Mankato, Minn.: Capstone Press, 2004.

INTERNET SITES

FactHound offers a safe, fun way to find Internet sites related to this book. All of the sites on FactHound have been researched by our staff.

Here's how:
1. Visit *www.facthound.com*
2. Choose your grade level.
3. Type in this book ID **0736864539** for age-appropriate sites. You may also browse subjects by clicking on letters, or by clicking on pictures and words.
4. Click on the **Fetch It** button.

FactHound will fetch the best sites for you!

INDEX